Think Write Book:
A Sentence Combining Workbook for ELL Students
(Student Edition)

www.thinkwritebook.com

by
Inès Millin Mevs

authorHOUSE®

AuthorHouse™
1663 Liberty Drive, Suite 200
Bloomington, IN 47403
www.authorhouse.com
Phone: 1-800-839-8640

©2008 Inès Millin Mevs. All rights reserved.

No part of this book may be reproduced, stored in a retrieval system, or transmitted by any means without the written permission of the author.

First published by AuthorHouse 1/2/2008

ISBN: 978-1-4343-4828-9 (e)
ISBN: 978-1-4343-4827-2 (sc)

Library of Congress Control Number: 2007910310

Printed in the United States of America
Bloomington, Indiana

This book is printed on acid-free paper.

Table of Contents

Dedication vii

For Students 1
    Analyzing and Evaluating Your Sentence Combinations 2
    Six basic qualities to consider when evaluating your new sentences: 2

Key Transition Words 3

Conjunctions and Other Key Words 5
    Coordinating Conjunctions 5
    Subordinating Conjunctions 5
    Correlative Conjunctions 5
    Relative Pronouns Used To Begin Dependent (Subordinate) Clauses 5

Examples For Sentence Combining Exercises 7
    Compound Sentences (With Coordinating Conjunctions) 7
    Complex Sentences (With Subordinating Conjunctions) 8
    One more thing 9

Sentence Combining Using Coordinating Conjunctions 11
    Connecting Sentence Elements – Part 1 & 2 11

Sentence Combining Using Coordinating Conjunctions 15
    Connecting Simple Sentences 15

Sentence Combining Using Subordinating Conjunctions 19
    Connecting Simple Sentences 19

More Practice with Combining Simple Sentences Into Complex Structures 21

Combining Sentences Showing Comparisons Using "More Than" + Gerunds 23

Combining Simple Sentences Into Compound and Complex Structures 25

Constructing Complex Sentences 29
    Combining Simple Sentences with Various Types of Dependent Clauses 29

How Many Wonders of the World Are There? 51
    Sentence Construction Exercise: Combining, Revising, and Editing 51

It's a first: Two Cat 5 Hurricanes Hit Land in 1 year! 59

Constructing Paragraphs Using Sentence Combining 69

Notes

Dedication

This book is dedicated to:

- all my students (present, past, and yet to come) – my courageous learners, my heroes, representing the future inside the four walls of my classroom
- my immediate family (world's best support system) – Simone, Jonah, Henry O., and Clotilda E.
- my parents, Angela and Henry A. – may they rest in peace
- my maternal and paternal grandparents, especially Lucinda, my first school teacher
- my teachers, professors, mentors, and colleagues
- my inner circle friends, who really know who they are, what they mean to me, and who know how deeply they are treasured
- my "Virgin Islands Homie," Patricia – a lovely, intelligent lady so full of grace and truth
- most of all, never last and never least, Rachel – my friend, my sister, and my confidante who kept on telling me: "You need to write the book that is in your head!"

"Our deepest fear is not that we are inadequate. Our deepest fear is that we are powerful beyond measure. It is our light, not our darkness, that most frightens us.' We ask ourselves, Who am I to be brilliant, gorgeous, talented, fabulous? Actually, who are you not to be?... Your playing small doesn't serve the world. There's nothing enlightened about shrinking so that other people won't feel insecure around you. We are all meant to shine, as children do... It's not just in some of us; it's in everyone. And as we let our own light shine, we subconsciously give other people permission to do the same. As we're liberated from our own fear, our presence automatically liberates others." (Marianne Williamson, author, from A Return To Love, 1992. Ack C Wilson and J Cooke.

"Don't be afraid to take a big step when one is indicated. You can't cross a chasm in two small steps." (David Lloyd George, 1863-1945, Welsh Liberal Statesman - with acknowledgements to Barbara Heyn.)

"We must become the change we want to see." (Mahatma Gandhi, 1869-1948, Indian statesman and spiritual leader, humanitarian and constitutional independence reformer – with acknowledgements to B Heyn.)

Notes

For Students

The primary purpose of this Think Write Book is to teach sentence construction along with revision, editing, and vocabulary skills through topics found in various content areas. Students will learn, practice, and fine tune their writing skills through the manipulation of words, groups of words, and simple sentences. The goal is to lead students to produce more complicated, logical, and fluent compound, complex, and compound-complex sentences, while learning specific content found in core curriculum courses, such as social studies, science, government, economics, technology, and much more.

The four sentence manipulatory skills to be learned through the practice exercises are:

1. Combining words, phrases, along with dependent and independent clauses
2. Rearranging words and other elements of clauses and simple sentences
3. Removing (or subtracting) words that are no longer necessary
4. Expanding (or adding) words and elements to make meaning and ideas more clear.

By mastering these skills, you will not only improve your syntax and fluency, but you will also acquire a stronger writer's vocabulary that will aid you in enhancing your overall written communication skills and academic writing assignments, which include composing and revising:

- Compositions (narrative, expository, descriptive, and persuasive essays),
- Book and film reports,
- Short and extended responses (on tests and other types of assessments), and
- Research papers.

The exercises in this workbook will introduce you to sentence combining--that is, organizing sets of short, choppy sentences into longer, more effective ones. However, the goal of sentence combining is not necessarily to produce *longer* sentences but rather to develop *more effective* sentences--and to help you become a more versatile writer.

Analyzing and Evaluating Your Sentence Combinations

After combining a set of sentences in a variety of ways, you should take time to evaluate your work and decide which combinations you like and which ones you don't. You can do this evaluation on your own, but there may be class sessions in which your teacher will direct you and your classmates to work in a group. This will give you opportunities to collaborate as a team, compare your new sentences with those of others, and assess your own progress. In either case, you should read your sentences out loud as you evaluate them, because how your sentences *sound* to you can be just as revealing and empowering as how they look.

There are six basic qualities to consider when you evaluate your new sentences: meaning, clarity, coherence, emphasis, conciseness, and rhythm. Below there are questions for you to consider for each of these qualities. They will help you to think more critically about your writing, which in turn will help you to fine-tune the final drafts of your sentences, paragraphs, and longer documents. The Key Transition Words chart below features some of the key words that can be used in constructing your combined sentences.

Six basic qualities to consider when evaluating your new sentences:

1. **Meaning.** As far as you can determine, have you conveyed the idea intended by the original author?
2. **Clarity.** Is the sentence clear? Can it be understood on the first reading?
3. **Coherence** Do the various parts of the sentence fit together logically and smoothly?
4. **Emphasis.** Are key words and phrases put in emphatic positions (usually at the very end or at the very beginning of the sentence)?
5. **Conciseness.** Does the sentence clearly express an idea without wasting words?
6. **Rhythm.** Does the sentence flow, or is it marked by awkward interruptions? Do the interruptions help to emphasize key points (an effective technique), or do they merely distract (an ineffective technique)?

These six qualities are so closely related that one can't be easily separated from another. The significance of the various qualities--and their interrelationship--should become clearer to you as you continue practicing.

Key Transition Words

One of the ways in which we can avoid producing choppy sentences and increase our sentence length and variety is to use transitional devices are words or phrases that help carry a thought from one sentence to another, from one idea to another, or from one paragraph to another. The following chart provides a list of words and phrases along with how they function within sentences and paragraphs.

Additions:	and	furthermore
	also	in addition
	for example	moreover
	for instance	
Parallels:	as	similarly
	just as	too
	likewise	
Contrasts:	alternatively	on the other hand
	although	not
	but	rather than
	by contrast	though
	despite	unless
	however	while
	in spite of	yet
Logic:	because	go
	before	then
	consequently	therefore
	for	thus
	if	until
	in conclusion	when
	since	where
	if . . . then	since . . . therefore
	so . . .	that such . . . that

Notes for Grammar Points

Conjunctions and Other Key Words

Coordinating Conjunctions
(There are seven sometimes called the FANBOYS, as a mnemonic device.)

<u>F</u>or   <u>A</u>nd   <u>N</u>or   <u>B</u>ut   <u>O</u>r   <u>Y</u>et   <u>S</u>o

Subordinating Conjunctions
(The following is a list of subordinating conjunctions and the relationships they express.)

Time relationships	Cause-effect relationships	Location	Contrast or Opposites	Conditional relationship
after	as	where	although	if
as	because	wherever	even though	even if
before	In order that		though	in case (that)
once	now that		whereas	unless
since	so		while	whether or not
until				
when				
whenever				
while				

Correlative Conjunctions
(These conjunctions travel in pairs, joining various sentence elements that should be treated as grammatically equal.)

as … as   either … or   not … but

both … and   neither … nor   not only … but also

whether … or

Relative Pronouns Used To Begin Dependent (Subordinate) Clauses

who   whom   whose   whoever   whomever

whosoever   that   whatever   which

Notes for Grammar Points

Examples For Sentence Combining Exercises

Compound Sentences (With Coordinating Conjunctions)

Simple sentences:

The United States of America was one hundred years old in 1876.

That same year, Pablo Casals was born in Spain.

(Use *and*.)

Combined sentences:

The United States of America was one hundred years old in 1876, <u>and</u> that same year, Pablo Casals was born in Spain.

Simple sentences:

Something happened just before Pablo's birth.

Alexander Graham Bell had invented the telephone.

People did not have telephones in their houses.

(Use *but*.)

Combined sentences:

Just before Pablo's birth, Alexander Graham Bell had invented the telephone, <u>but</u> people did not have telephones in their houses.

Simple sentences:

Roberto Clemente was born in Carolina, Puerto Rico.

This happened in 1934.

He was a baseball hero.

(Use *and*.)

Combined sentences:

Roberto Clemente was born in Carolina, Puerto Rico in 1934, <u>and</u> he was a baseball hero.

Complex Sentences (With Subordinating Conjunctions)

Simple sentences:

I like ripe strawberries.

Ripe strawberries are very tasty.

Ripe strawberries are very nutritious.

(Use *because*.)

Combined sentences:

I like ripe strawberries because they are very tasty and nutritious.

Simple sentences:

I like strawberries.

Strawberries are covered with chocolate.

I like strawberries covered with chocolate even more.

(Use *although* and *when*.)

Combined sentences:

Although I like strawberries, I like them even more when they are chocolate-covered.

Simple sentences:

I enjoyed watching the sunrise today.

The sunrise was very beautiful today.

The sky was cloudless.

The colors were magnificent.

[Use ; (a semi-colon). Use *and*.]

Combined sentences:

I enjoyed watching the very beautiful sunrise today; the sky was cloudless, and the colors were magnificent.

One more thing

As you move forward with your practice exercises in this workbook, there is a simple rubric that you can use to assess your sentences, paragraphs, and even longer documents, such as book reports and research papers. After writing your first draft sentences and paragraphs, you will need to analyze them and think of ways that can begin revising, editing, and fine-tuning your sentences. This rubric is called **COPS**, which is an acronym for:

Capital letters

Order of words

Punctuation, and

Spelling.

A writing rubric is a scoring tool (a way to measure) the criteria for your writing. Criteria are the accepted standards that are used in making decision or judgments about your writing performance. In your English and Language Arts classes, your teacher will probably discuss the elements and details of writing rubrics, especially when you take standardized tests that require you to write a response to a prompt. Your teachers also use rubrics to score your writing assignments, and you will probably use rubrics when you read your classmates' writing. The important thing for you to remember is the following: If you know what is expected of your writing, the better experience you will have as you work through the process of constructing, revising, editing and refining your writing, and other people's writing as well. Improving your writing will also greatly improve your reading and thinking skills – think of this as a bonus that will strengthen your communication and academic skills for your other classes (such as math, science, social studies, and more).

Notes for Grammar Points

Sentence Combining Using Coordinating Conjunctions

Connecting Sentence Elements – Part 1 & 2

Created by: Inès M. Mevs, M.S.Ed.

Part 1:

DIRECTIONS: Read each pair of simple sentences. Combine each pair of sentences into one sentence by using the conjunction **and**. You may need to make other changes to your sentences, so that they are logical and correct. Be sure to use **COPS** – correct capital letters, order of words, punctuation, and spelling.

1. Architects design buildings. Architects design parks.

    _____

    _____

    _____

2. Architects find out about the environment. Architects find out about the people there.

    _____

    _____

    _____

3. Buildings provide us with a place to eat. Buildings provide us with a place to sleep.

    _____

    _____

    _____

4. Buildings protect us from rain. Buildings protect us from snow.

_____

_____

_____

5. In the 1800s people traveled on foot. In the 1800s people traveled on horseback.

_____

_____

_____

6. Today in 2007 we have electricity. Today in 2007 we have cell phones.

_____

_____

_____

7. We have lap top computers. We have lots of other great technology.

_____

_____

_____

Part 2:

DIRECTIONS: Read each pair of simple sentences. Combine each pair of sentences into one sentence by using the conjunction **or**. You may need to make other changes to your sentences, so that they are logical and correct. Be sure to use **COPS** – correct capital letters, order of words, punctuation, and spelling.

8. In the early 1800s there were no electric lights. In the early 1800s there were no refrigerators.

_____

_____

_____

9. In the early 1800s people traveled on horseback. In the early 1800s people traveled by horse-drawn carriage.

_____

_____

10. There were no airplanes. There were no space shuttles.

_____

_____

11. There were no telephones. There were no iPods.

_____

_____

12. People didn't have cars. People didn't have flat screen televisions.

_____

_____

13. Today in 2007 we don't need to walk. Today in 2007 we don't need to suffer from heat.

_____

_____

14. We can go see a movie in the theater. We can rent movies to enjoy at home.

_____

_____

Notes for Grammar Points

Sentence Combining Using Coordinating Conjunctions

Connecting Simple Sentences

Created by: Inès M. Mevs, M.S.Ed.

DIRECTIONS: Read each pair or group of simple sentences carefully. Think about how to combine the ideas of each sentence in the pairs or groups by eliminating words that are repeated or are more than necessary. Rewrite each pair or group of sentences into compound sentences that are smooth and logical. You will need to use coordinating conjunctions to connect ideas, and you may need to replace some nouns with pronouns. Some compound sentences may need semicolons. Remember to use **COPS**.

1. Pablo Casals had extraordinary talent.

    Pablo Casals could play several musical instruments.

    Pablo Casals could play the flute, piano, organ, violin, and cello.

    [Use **a semicolon (;). / such as**]

    _____

    _____

    _____

2. Roberto joined his first neighborhood baseball team.

    This happened at the age of 8.

    Something happened ten years later.

    This happened at age 18.

    He signed his first professional baseball contract.

    The contract was with the Santurce team.

    The team was in the Puerto Rico Winter League.

    [Use **a semicolon (;).**]

15

_____

_____

_____

3. Betty Marie Tall Chief was a Native American.
   Betty Marie Tall Chief was born on the Osage Reservation.
   The Osage Reservation was in Fairfax, Oklahoma.
   Betty Marie Tall Chief was a dancer.
   Betty Marie Tall Chief was American-born.
   Betty Marie Tall Chief was the first dancer with a title.
   Betty Marie Tall Chief had the title of "prima ballerina."
   (Use **and**.)

_____

_____

_____

4. Betty Marie had a great-grandfather.
   He was very important.
   He was Peter Bigheart.
   He was an Osage chief.
   [Use **a semicolon (;)**.]

_____

_____

_____

5. Something happened by the end of Betty Marie's performing career.
   Betty Marie had danced with all the important U.S. ballet companies.
   She had performed all over the world.
   [Use **and**.]

_____
_____
_____

Notes for Grammar Points

Sentence Combining Using Subordinating Conjunctions

Connecting Simple Sentences

Created by: Inès M. Mevs, M.S.Ed.

DIRECTIONS: Read each pair or group of simple sentences carefully. Think about how to combine the ideas of each sentence in the pairs or groups by eliminating words that are repeated or are more than necessary. Rewrite each pair or group of sentences into complex sentences that are smooth and logical. You will need to use subordinating conjunctions to connect ideas, and you may need to replace some nouns with pronouns. Remember to use **COPS**.

1. Pablo Casals was a man.

   Pablo Casals was remarkable.

   Pablo Casals lived for almost one hundred years.

   (Use **who**.)

   _____

   _____

   _____

2. World War II ended in 1945.

   Pablo Casals had expected an end to something.

   There was the dictatorship in Spain.

   (Use **when**.)

   _____

   _____

   _____

3. Pablo Casals expected support for freedom in Spain.

   The support was from other democratic countries.

   The support did not happen.

   Pablo Casals refused public performances in those countries.

   [Use a **semicolon** (;). / **because**]

   _____

   _____

   _____

4. Roberto Clemente wanted a chance.

   Roberto Clemente wanted to play baseball in one of the U.S. major leagues.

   The U.S. major leagues are the National League and the American League.

   (Use **which**.)

   _____

   _____

   _____

5 Roberto Clemente signed a contract.

   The contract was with the Brooklyn Dodgers.

   Roberto Clemente was sent to the Brooklyn Dodger's farm team.

   The farm team was in Montreal, Canada.

   (Use **when**.)

   _____

   _____

   _____

6. The Native Americans could travel only on foot or by boat.

   Then the Spaniards came.

   (Use **before**.)

   _____

   _____

More Practice with Combining Simple Sentences Into Complex Structures

Created by: Inès M. Mevs, M.S.Ed.

DIRECTIONS: Read each pair or group of simple sentences carefully. Think about how to combine the ideas of each sentence in the pairs or groups by eliminating words that are repeated or are more than necessary. Rewrite each pair or group of sentences complex sentences that are smooth and logical. You will need to use subordinating conjunctions to connect ideas. You may need to replace some nouns with pronouns. Remember to use **COPS**.

1. You can't fish in this lake. You must have a license. (Use **unless**.)

_____

_____

_____

2. It is raining. It is useless to wash my car. (Use **while**.)

_____

_____

_____

3. The game will end soon. Let's start to leave. (Use **as**.)

_____

_____

_____

4. I can't buy a new tire for my car. I don't have enough money. (Use **because**.)

_____

_____

5. You are overweight. You should diet. (Use **if**.)

_____

_____

6. The marathon will begin. The starter gives the signal. (Use **when**.)

_____

_____

7. We scored eight touchdowns. We did not win the game. (Use **although**.)

_____

_____

8. We are very happy. We get to sleep later on late start days at school. (Use **whenever**.)

_____

_____

Combining Sentences Showing Comparisons Using "More Than" + Gerunds

Created by: Inès M. Mevs, M.S.Ed.

DIRECTIONS: Read each pair or group of simple sentences carefully. Think about how to combine the ideas of each sentence in the pairs or groups by eliminating words that are repeated or are more than necessary. Rewrite each pair or group of sentences into one sentence that shows a comparison using "more than" with gerunds/gerund phrases. You may also need to replace some nouns with pronouns. Remember to use **COPS**.

1. Betty Marie Tall Chief liked playing the piano.
   Betty Marie Tall Chief also liked dancing.
   Betty Marie Tall Chief liked dancing more.

   _____

   _____

   _____

2. Pedro likes riding a bicycle.
   Pedro also likes rollerblading.
   Pedro prefers rollerblading more.

   _____

   _____

   _____

3. I like watching television.
   I also like listening to music.
   I like watching television more.

4. Janet likes reading books.
   Janet likes writing poems.
   Janet likes reading books more.

5. Understanding Algebra 2 is difficult for me.
   Understanding chemistry is also difficult for me.
   Understanding chemistry is more difficult.

6. Cooking dinner on a barbecue grill can be dangerous.
   Cooking dinner on a gas stove can also be dangerous.
   Cooking dinner on a barbecue grill is more dangerous.

Combining Simple Sentences Into Compound and Complex Structures

Created by: Inès M. Mevs, M.S.Ed.

DIRECTIONS: Read each pair or group of simple sentences carefully. Think about how to combine the ideas of each sentence in the pairs or groups by eliminating words that are repeated or are more than necessary. Rewrite each pair or group of sentences into compound, complex, or compound-complex sentences that are smooth and logical. You may need to use coordinating and/or subordinating conjunctions to connect ideas. You may need to replace some nouns with pronouns. Some compound and compound-complex sentences may need semicolons. Remember to use **COPS**.

1. Our neighbors are moving to North Carolina.
   Our neighbors' house is for sale.

   _____

   _____

   _____

2. Our English teacher, Ms. Mevs, usually has a good sense of humor.
   Our English teacher was not amused by the practical joke.

   _____

   _____

   _____

3. The sweater had been knitted by my Aunt Rosie.
   My mother wore the sweater to the football game.

   _____

   _____

4. Joseph has a bedroom all to himself now.
   Joseph's brother is away at college.
   _____
   _____
   _____

5. The library is the only place where Ariana can study.
   The library has been closed for three weeks due to a leaky roof.
   _____
   _____
   _____

6. Carlos is the fastest runner in the class.
   Carlos has set the school record in the 100 yard dash.
   _____
   _____
   _____

7. George Washington Carver was a brilliant scientist.
   George Washington Carver made over 300 products from the peanut.
   _____
   _____
   _____

8. Sarah had to finish the term paper by tomorrow night.
   Sarah had a broken computer.
   _____
   _____
   _____
   _____

9. Our teacher used to live in Greece.

   Our teacher is very fond of Greek food.

   _____

   _____

   _____

10. The map was printed during World War II.

    The map is older than your parents.

    _____

    _____

    _____

11. Evelyn was terribly interested in the histories of capitals of countries all around the world.

    Evelyn had often heard that her great-grandfather toured in most of the capitals of countries in South America.

    _____

    _____

    _____

12. Thanksgiving Day is an American holiday.

    Thanksgiving Day is celebrated in November.

    _____

    _____

    _____

13. A bulletin board is on one wall of the classroom.

    A bulletin board has various posters and students' papers.

    _____

    _____

    _____

14. The Seven-Mile Bridge is one of the many bridges on US 1 in the Florida Keys. The Seven-Mile Bridge is among the longest bridges in existence.

_____

_____

_____

Constructing Complex Sentences

Combining Simple Sentences with Various Types of Dependent Clauses

Created by: Inès M. Mevs, M.S.Ed.

DIRECTIONS: Read the following sets of sentences carefully. Under each set there is a direction (in parentheses) that gives a suggested coordinating and/or subordinating conjunction (in **bold print**), and where they should be placed. Using the suggested conjunctions, combine each group of sentences into one complex sentence. Some sentences are actually compound-complex. Be sure to make your sentences smooth and logical. Watch out for **COPS** (**capital letters, order of words, punctuation, and spelling**)

1. Ripe mangos splattered from the tree. No one had picked them.

    (Use **because**/2ND sentence)

    _____
    _____
    _____

2. The breeze blew lightly. The bees buzzed crazily in circles.

    (Use **as**/1ST sentence)

    _____
    _____
    _____

3. The young man was napping and dreaming happy dreams. The young man smiled and snored.

    (Use **because**/1ST sentence)

    _____
    _____

4. Unfortunately, he was resting on an anthill. The anthill was full of fire ants.
   (Use that/2ND sentence)

5. The dreamer didn't know it. The ants were very upset.
   (Use **that**/2ND sentence.)

6. The ants plotted their revenge. The ants imagined fresh meat for dinner.
   (Use **while**/2ND sentence.)

7. The Chargers have no quarterback. The Chargers have no chance of going to the playoffs this year.
   Use **because**/1ST sentence.)

8. After a touchdown, special teams in football often are responsible for the extra points. The extra points mean the difference between winning and losing.
   (Use **that**/2ND sentence.)

9. The players come into the locker room after a game. The players shower and get dressed to go home.

   (Use **when**/1ˢᵀ sentence.)

   _____

   _____

   _____

10. A tsunami can be up to several hundred miles long. Sometimes a tsunami's waves may be only three feet high.

    (Use **although**/1ˢᵀ sentence.)

    _____

    _____

    _____

11. The waves may be only three feet high. The waves may be very difficult to detect.

    (Use **because**/1ˢᵀ sentence.)

    _____

    _____

    _____

12. A nearby ship might not notice a tsunami. A tsunami is only three feet high.

    (Use **that**/2ᴺᴰ sentence.)

    _____

    _____

    _____

13. The tsunami reaches shallow water near the coast. The height of the wave is amplified.

    (Use **when**/1ˢᵀ sentences.)

    _____

    _____

14. The new school year starts. You can sleep until ten in the mornings.
    (Use **until**/1ST sentence.)
    _____
    _____
    _____

15. You had better get your work done. Your work is due.
    (Use **before**/2ND sentence)
    _____
    _____
    _____

16. You had better get your work done. It's too late to turn it in for credit.
    (Use **before**/2ND sentence.)
    _____
    _____
    _____

17. Your teacher is heartless. You have no chance to pass this class. You work hard.
    (Use **since**/1ST sentence.) (Use unless/3RD sentence.)
    _____
    _____
    _____

18. You are a hard worker. Your teachers admire you.
    (Use **because**/1ST sentence.)
    _____
    _____
    _____

19. You want free time after school. You should finish your homework quickly and completely.

    (Use **if**/1ˢᵀ sentence.)

    _____

    _____

    _____

20. My teacher is in a foul mood. He gives tons of homework.

    (Use **whenever**/1ˢᵀ sentence.)

    _____

    _____

    _____

21. The thunder crashed. The sky were exploding.

    (Use **as if**/ 2ᴺᴰ sentence.)

    _____

    _____

    _____

22. I love my slippers. They tickle my toes.

    (Use **because**/2ᴺᴰ sentence.)

    _____

    _____

    _____

23. You get sunburned. You increase your risk of skin cancer.

    (Use **when**/1ˢᵀ sentence.)

    _____

    _____

    _____

24. An urban myth tells us something. Ninety percent of our brain is unused.
    (Use **that**/2^(ND) sentence.)

25. This might not be true for all of us. Most of us do have some extra spots in our brains. Extra spots are available for a few random facts and bits of information.
    (Use **but**/2^(ND) sentence.) (Use **that**/3^(RD) sentence.)

26. The fact exists. Snails can sleep for three years without eating is amazing.
    Use **that**/2^(ND) sentence.)

27. Around my house, snails don't live that long.   I am the garden snails' chief archenemy.
    (Use **because**/2^(ND) sentence.)

28. There is another fascinating fact.   Koala bears' fingerprints are virtually indistinguishable from human prints. They could be confused at a crime scene.
    (Use **that**/2^(ND) sentence.) (Use **so**/3^(RD) sentence.)

29. Did you know something?   An ostrich's eyeball is bigger than its brain.

(Use **that**/2ᴺᴰ sentence.)

_____

_____

_____

30. An ostrich's eyeball is also bigger than many people's brains. People's actions are any indication of brain size.

(Use **if**/2ᴺᴰ sentence.)

_____

_____

_____

31. Anna is not the only student. The teacher gave an "A" to Anna..

Use **to whom**/2ᴺᴰ sentence.)

_____

_____

_____

32. Gabriela was embarrassed by a remark. The remark was unkind.

(Use **that**/2ᴺᴰ sentence.

_____

_____

_____

33. The boy was very cold that night. The boy's jacket was lost.

(Use **whose**, insert in 1ˢᵀ sentence.)

_____

_____

_____

34. The helicopters flew over the citizens. The citizens were irate.

(Use **whom**, insert in 2ND sentence.)

35. The kids were at the football game. The kids came home. The whole family ate.

(Use **after**/1ST sentence.) (Use **who**, insert in 1ST sentence.)

36. The dusty puppies were under the bed. The dusty puppies were as big as Great Danes.

(Use **which**/1ST sentence.)

37. The Lock Ness monster lives supposedly in the lake. The lake is very deep.

(Use **which**/1ST sentence.)

38. The detective found the prints. The detective was careless with the evidence.

(Use **who**/1ST sentence.)

39. The detective shot the criminal. The criminal was wanted in three states.

   (Use **whom**/1st sentence.)

40. The detective investigated the crime scene with his partner. His partner was crooked.

   (Use **whom**/1ST sentence.)

41. The policeman was incompetent. The detective gave the evidence to the policeman.

   (Use **whom**/1ST sentence.)

42. I believe something. The witness testified about the gun. The witness was lying.

   (Use **that**/2ND sentence.) (Use **who**/2ND sentence).

43. The detective arrested a thief. The detective caught a thief red-handed.

   (Use **whom**/2ND sentence.)

44. The baseball pitcher got the two-year contract. The pitcher broke his arm.

(Use **who**/1ST sentence

45. You sent the card to my friend. My friend feels better.

(Use **whom**/1ST sentence.)

46. I sent a letter to the man. The letter described my situation. The overcharged me.

(Use **that**/2ND sentence.) Use **who**/3RD sentence.)

47. Teachers are much more astute. Their students expect them to be.

(Use **than**/2ND sentence.)

48. An incident occurred several years ago at Duke University. The incident illustrates this.

(Use **that**/2ND sentence.)

49. The night before final exams, two students decided to go to a party at another college. The college was some distance away.

Use **that**/2^(ND) sentence.)

_____

_____

_____

50. College students sometimes do something. College students spend the whole at the party.

This fun-loving pair spent the whole night at the party. This fun-loving pair did not make the long drive back to their dormitory.

(Use **as**/1^(ST) sentence.) (Use **and**/4^(TH) sentence.)

_____

_____

_____

_____

51. Unfortunately, the next morning they realized something. They had missed their exam.

(Use **that**/2^(ND) sentence.)

_____

_____

_____

52. To avoid failing, they decided to concoct an excuse about something. They were returning to campus. They got a flat tire.

(Use **how**/2^(ND) sentence.) (Use **when**/3^(RD) sentence.)

_____

_____

_____

_____

53. They told the professor their sad tale. The professor seemed very sympathetic. The professor gave them permission to take the exam the next day.

(Use **whom**/1ST sentence.) (Use **and**/3RD sentence.)

_____

_____

_____

54. The two students got some rest. The two students showed up the next day to take their exam.

(Use **after**/1ST sentence.)

_____

_____

_____

55. The professor gave each of them a copy of the exam. The professor sent them into two separate rooms to take the exam.

(Use **after**/1ST sentence.)

_____

_____

_____

56. The two students were both surprised the exam. The exam was short with just two questions.

(Use **because**/2ND sentence.)

_____

_____

_____

57. The first question was very difficult to answer. The second question was even harder.

(Use **although**/1ST sentence.)

_____

_____

58. The two students were surprised. The second question asked: "Which tire?"
    (Use **because**/2ND sentence.)

59. I will give my leftovers to someone. Someone wants them.
    (Use **whoever**/2ND sentence.)

60. You are someone. Someone makes no difference to me.
    (Use **who**/1ST sentence.)

61. Young readers think something. The Harry Potter books are the best new series.
    (Use **that**/2ND sentence.)

62. Computers can do something. It is unbelievable.
    (Use **what**/1ST sentence.)

63. Surfing can be dangerous. Surfing is worth the risk.

（Use **although**/1ˢᵀ sentence.)

_____

_____

_____

64. I surf. I get good exercise.

（Use **when**/1ˢᵀ sentence.)

_____

_____

_____

65. I go to the beach every weekend. It is stormy.

（Use **unless**/ 2ᴺᴰ sentence.)

_____

_____

_____

66. After a long day at work, a dip in the ocean is refreshing. It clears my mind.

（Use **because**/2ᴺᴰ sentence.)

_____

_____

_____

67. I get a rush. I see a huge wave bearing down on me. My adrenaline starts to pump.

（Use **when**/2ᴺᴰ sentence.) (Use **and**/3ᴿᴰ sentence.)

_____

_____

_____

_____

68. I don't believe in destiny. I am convinced. We were meant to be together.
(Use **although**/1ST sentence.) (Use **that**/3RD sentence.)

69. Karma means something. You do something. Something comes back to you.
(Use **that**/1ST sentence.) (Use **what**/2ND sentence.)

70. You are cruel to others. Others will be cruel to you.
(Use **if**/1ST sentence.)

71. I was an evil person in my last life. I don't deserve the predicament. I am in the predicament now.
(Use **unless**/1ST sentence.) (Use **that**/3RD sentence.)

72. Give the raise to someone. Someone deserves the raise.
(Use **whoever**/2ND sentence.)

73. The treasurer was George's best friend. George still believed something. The money was handled carelessly.

(Use **although** 1ˢᵀ sentence.) (Use **that**/3ᴿᴰ sentence.)

___

___

___

74. Pranks require great engineering skill. Pranks cause no damage. Pranks are legendary at Massachusetts Institute of Technology.

(Use **that**/1ˢᵀ sentence.) (Use **but**/2ᴺᴰ sentence.)

___

___

___

75. My parents complain. I am the laziest person in the family.

(Use **that**/2ᴺᴰ sentence.)

___

___

___

76. I would feel more relaxed. I had finished my science project.

(Use **if**/2ᴺᴰ sentence.)

___

___

___

77. There was a dead whale. A dead whale had washed up on the beach last month.

(Use **that**/2ᴺᴰ sentence.)

___

___

___

44

78. I washed my hair. I finished my homework.

(Use **after**/2ND sentence.)

79. The soup is simmering on the stove. The soup smells fragrant.

(Use **that**/1ST sentence.)

80. Wrapped in an old shawl, the elderly man carried a smelly fish. He had caught a smelly fish in the river.

(Use **that**/2ND sentence.)

81. You should stretch your muscles. You exercise. It is important.

(Use **before**/2ND sentence.) (Use **because**/3RD sentence.)

82. The Atlanta Braves baseball team tried to slip into first place. The New York Mets ball club was unstoppable.

(Use **although**/1ST sentence.)

83. I like to go the beach after a storm. The waves are spectacular.

(Use **because**/ 2ND sentence.)

___

84. A storm threatens. You should have a flashlight, some bottled water, and a first aid kit.

(Use **if**/1ST sentence.)

___

85. The states have been extensively damaged by hurricanes in recent years. The states are:

North Carolina, Texas, South Carolina, Georgia, and Florida.

(Use **that**/1ST sentence.)

___

86. Mr. Smith had been driving for 50 years. Mr. Smith had his first traffic accident.

(Use **after**/1ST sentence.)

___

87. We need someone to care for our puppy for two days. Someone does not smoke or drink.

(Use **who**/1ST sentence.)

88. Nothing beats a hot dog. A hot dog is slathered with ketchup, mustard, and sauerkraut.

(Use **that**/2ND sentence.)

89. The dogs were barking. The dogs made a racket.

(Use **that**/2ND sentence.)

90. I was a hero. I would rush into that burning building.

(Use **if**/1ST sentence.)

91. The black employee was fired. At one time discrimination was still legal.

(Use **when**/2ND sentence.) (Change **one** to **a**.)

92. It is raining. We can stay warm and cozy inside the house.

(Use **since**/1ST sentence.)

93. The sun was out. We could have a picnic.

   (Use **if**/1ˢᵀ sentence.)

   _____

   _____

   _____

94. You have learned to hum the melody. The lyrics are easy to memorize.

   (Use **after**/1ˢᵀ sentence.)

   _____

   _____

   _____

95. I turned eight. My mother gave me my own encyclopedia.

   (Use **when**/1ˢᵀ sentence.)

   _____

   _____

   _____

96. Fire-walking gurus claim something. Your mind can control matter.

   (Use **that**/2ⁿᴅ sentence.)

   _____

   _____

   _____

97. For a not-so-small fee, these gurus can teach you something.   You can harness the untapped power of your mind.

   (Use **how**/2ⁿᴅ sentence.)

   _____

   _____

   _____

   _____

98. One is faced with a bowl of potato chips. It is difficult to learn self-control.

   (Use **when**/1ST sentence.)

   _____

   _____

   _____

99. I also find it difficult to control myself. I see guacamole.

   (Use **when**/2ND sentence.)

   _____

   _____

   _____

100. I find it most difficult to exert self-control. I am passing by an ice cream parlor on a hot day.

   (Use **when**/2ND sentence.)

   _____

   _____

   _____

Notes for Grammar Points

How Many Wonders of the World Are There?

Sentence Construction Exercise: Combining, Revising, and Editing

Created by: Inès M. Mevs, M.S.Ed.

DIRECTIONS: Read each set of simple sentences carefully. Think about how to combine the ideas of each sentence in the pairs or groups by eliminating words that are repeated more than necessary. Rewrite each pair or group of sentences into compound, complex, or compound-complex sentences that are smooth and logical. You may need to use coordinating and/or subordinating conjunctions to connect ideas. You may need to replace some nouns with pronouns. Some compound and compound-complex sentences may need semicolons. Remember to use **COPS**.

1. Most people know of a list of the Seven World Wonders.
   Most people cannot name them.

   _____
   _____
   _____
   _____

2. The task of compiling the Seven Wonders of the World for people would have been really a tough one.
   There were so many marvels to choose from.

   _____
   _____
   _____
   _____

3. The final list of the Seven Wonders was compiled during the Middle Ages.

   The list comprised the seven most impressive monuments of the Ancient World.

   _____

   _____

   _____

4. For their builders, the Seven Wonders were a celebration of religion, mythology, art, power, and science.

   For us, they reflect the ability of humans to change the surrounding landscape by building massive yet beautiful structures.

   _____

   _____

   _____

5. There are other lists of "Seven Wonders" of the world.

   There is even a list of the "Forgotten Wonders of the World."

   The list of the "Forgotten Wonders of the World" includes twelve geographical locations.

   _____

   _____

   _____

6. There is a list of "The Seven Wonders of the Ancient World."

   The list of "The Seven Wonders of the Ancient World" includes the Gread Pyramid of Giza.

   The list of "The Seven Wonders of the Ancient World" includes the Hanging Gardens of Babylon.

   The list of "The Seven Wonders of the Ancient World" includes the Temple of Artemis at Ephesus.

   The list of "The Seven Wonders of the Ancient World" includes the Statue of Zeus at Olympia.

   The list of "The Seven Wonders of the Ancient World" includes the Mausoleum at Halicarnassus.

The list of "The Seven Wonders of the Ancient World" includes the Colossus of Rhodes.

The list of "The Seven Wonders of the Ancient World" includes the Pharos of Alexandria.

_____

_____

_____

_____

7 There is also a list of "The Seven Wonders of the Medieval Mind."

The list of "The Seven Wonders of the Medieval Mind" includes Stonehenge.

The list of "The Seven Wonders of the Medieval Mind" includes the Coliseum.

The list of "The Seven Wonders of the Medieval Mind" includes the Catacombs of Kom el Shoqafa.

The list of "The Seven Wonders of the Medieval Mind" includes the Great Wall of China.

The list of "The Seven Wonders of the Medieval Mind" includes the Porcelain Tower of Nanjing.

The list of "The Seven Wonders of the Medieval Mind" includes the Hagia Sophia.

The list of "The Seven Wonders of the Medieval Mind" includes the Leaning Tower of Pisa.

_____

_____

_____

_____

8. The "Seven Natural Wonders of the World" is another list of geographical locations.

Included on the list of the "Seven Natural Wonders of the World" is Mount Everest.

The Great Barrier Reef and the Grand Canyon are included on this list.

Victoria Falls and the Harbor of Rio de Janerio are also included on this list.

The list of the "Seven Natural Wonders of the World" also includes Paricutin Volcano and Northern Lights.

___

9. Not all wonders of the world are on land.

    There are locations on a list of "The Seven Underwater Wonders of the World."

    Three locations on this list are: Palau, the Belize Barrier Reef, and the Galapagos Islands.

    The other four locations on the list of "The Seven Underwater Wonders of the World" are the following: the Northern Red Sea, Lake Baikal, the Great Barrier Reef, and the Deep Sea Vents.

___

10. There are marvels of more modern human ingenuity around the world.

    There are seven identified locations on the list of "The Seven Wonders of the Modern World."

    One identified location on the list of "The Seven Wonders of the Modern World" is the Empire State Building.

    Other locations on this list include: the Itaipú Dam, the CN Tower, the Panama Canal, and the Channel Tunnel.

    The last two locations on the list of "The Seven Wonders of the Modern World" are the Netherland North Sea Protection Works and the Golden Gate Bridge.

11. Another group of wonders is the "Seven Forgotten Natural Wonders of the World."

    The list is comprised of seven locations.

    Angel Falls, Iguaçú Falls, and Niagara Falls are three of the "Seven Forgotten Natural Wonders of the World."

    The Bay of Fundy is another location in the list of the "Seven Forgotten Natural Wonders of the World."

    The other three locations on this list are Krakatoa Island, Mount Fuji, and Mount Kilimanjaro.

    _____
    _____
    _____

12. Seven more locations make up a list of the "Seven Forgotten Modern Wonders of the World."

    Two of these locations are the Aswan High Dam and the Hoover Dam.

    Included in this list are the Clock Tower (Big Ben), the Eiffel Tower, the Petronas Towers, and the Gateway Arch.

    The last location on this list is the Mount Rushmore National Memorial.

    _____
    _____
    _____

13. The Seven Forgotten Natural Wonders and the Seven Forgotten Modern Wonders are only two of the "forgotten" categories of world marvels.

    There is a third "forgotten" category.

    The third "forgotten" category is the "Seven Forgotten Wonders of the Medieval Mind."

    Five of the locations in this category are: the Abu Simbel Temple, Angkor Wat, the Taj Mahal, Mont Saint-Michel, and The Moai Statues.

    The other two locations are the Parthenon and the Shwedagon Pagoda.

    _____
    _____
    _____

14. Then there is a category of twelve locations.

    This category is simply called "The Forgotten Wonders."

    There are twelve world-wide locations on the list of "The Forgotten Wonders."

    The Aztec Temple, the Banaue Rice Terraces, the Borobudur Temple, and the Inca City are four of "The Forgotten Wonders."

    Also included in this category are the Statue of Liberty, the Mayan Temples, the Temple of the Inscriptions, and the Throne Hall of Persepolis.

    The last four locations of "The Forgotten Wonders" are Petra, the Suez Canal, the Sydney Opera House, and the Red Fort in India.

    _____
    _____
    _____

15. Recently, a contest was organized by the New7Wonders Foundation to decide a new list of human-made marvels.

    In July, 2007 seven "new wonders of the world" were announced.

    _____
    _____
    _____

16. The winners of the contest were voted for by Internet and phone, *American Idol* style.

    Among the "new seven wonders of the world" was the 105-foot-tall (38-meter-tall) "Christ the Redeemer" statue in Rio de Janeiro, Brazil.

    _____
    _____
    _____

17. There were six other "new wonders" of the world.

    The Colosseum in Rome is a "new wonder of the world."

    The Taj Mahal in India is a "new wonder of the world."

    The Great Wall of China is a "new wonder of the world."

The ancient city of Petra in Jordan is a "new wonder of the world."

The Inca ruins of Machu Picchu in Peru is a "new wonder of the world."

The ancient Mayan city of Chichén Itzá in Mexico is a "new wonder of the world."

_____

_____

_____

18. Yet the competition has proved controversial.

    The competition is drawing criticism from the United Nations' cultural organization UNESCO.

    UNESCO administers the World Heritage sites program.

    _____

    _____

    _____

19. The state of Florida has seven natural wonders.

    Visit Florida, Florida's official tourism site, has named "Florida's Seven Great Natural Wonders."

    _____

    _____

    _____

20. One location on the list "Florida's Seven Great Natural Wonders" is the Gulf Islands National Seashore.

    Another location of "Florida's Seven Great Natural Wonders" is the Timucuan Ecological and Historic Preserve.

    There are five other locations on the list of "Florida's Seven Great Natural Wonders" are the St. Johns River, the Kissimmee Prairie Preserve State Park, Lake Okeechobee, the Everglades National Park, and The Florida Reef.

    _____

    _____

    _____

Notes for Grammar Points

It's a first: Two Cat 5 Hurricanes Hit Land in 1 year!

Adapted from an article by Ken Kaye, reporter/writer for the South Florida Sun-Sentinel

8:32 AM EDT, September 5, 2007

DIRECTIONS: Read the following groups of simple sentences. Think about how to combine the ideas of each sentence in the groups by eliminating words that are repeated more than necessary. Think about how you can combine two or more of these sentences into longer compound, complex, and compound-complex sentences. You may need to use coordinating and/or subordinating conjunctions to connect ideas. You may need to replace some nouns with pronouns. Some compound and compound-complex sentences may need semicolons. Remember to use **COPS**.

1. Something happened on September 4, 2007.

   September 4, 2007 was on a Tuesday.

   Hurricane Felix was mighty.

   Hurricane Felix thundered ashore over a patch of jungle.

   The patch of jungle is remote.

   The patch of jungle is in Nicaragua.

   Hurricane Felix made tropical history.

   (when)

   _____

   _____

   _____

2. Something had never happened before in the annals of meteorology.

   Two hurricanes reached land in the same season.

   The two hurricanes were Category 5 hurricanes.

The two hurricanes were potentially catastrophic.

Hurricane Dean hit the same general area.

The general area is at the end of the Caribbean.

Hurricane Dean hit just 14 days earlier.

(as)

_____

_____

_____

3. Dennis Feltgen is a spokesman.

   Dennis Feltgen speaks for the National Hurricane Center.

   The National Hurricane Center is in Miami-Dade County.

   Dennis Feltgen said something.

   Such a weather event is "unprecedented".

   (who / that)

_____

_____

_____

4. Something is even more interesting.

   It was the first time.

   The first two hurricanes of a storm season reached certain strength.

   The strength was Category 5.

   Weather records started to be kept in 1851.

   The weather was tropical.

   (that / that / since)

_____

_____

_____

_____

5. All of that wasn't unusual.

   All of that wasn't enough.

   Dean followed tracks across the Caribbean.

   Felix followed tracks across the Caribbean.

   The tracks were almost parallel.

   Dean was making landfall.

   Felix was making landfall.

   The landfalls were within 550 miles of one another.

   (**if** / Change **wasn't** to **weren't**. / **and**)

   _____

   _____

   _____

6. Dean struck land.

   The land was near Chetumal.

   Chetumal is on Mexico's Yucatan.

   This happened on August 21.

   Dean left at least 20 people dead.

   Dean left billions of dollars in property damage.

   The damage was in Dean's wake.

   Both hurricanes had 165 mph winds at their peak.

   The winds were sustained.

   (Change **left** to present participle form. / **and** / ;)

   _____

   _____

   _____

7. There was yet another weather event.

   There was no known precedent.

   Something happened on Tuesday.

   There was a hurricane spawned in the Pacific.

The hurricane was Hurricane Henriette.

Hurricane Henriette rammed into resort areas.

The resort areas are on the tip of Baja California.

(Begin with **and**. / Use **with**. / **:**)

_____

_____

_____

8. It was the first time.

   Atlantic hurricanes made landfall.

   Pacific hurricanes made landfall.

   Hurricanes made landfall on the same day.

   The hurricane center began keeping records.

   The records were of storms in 1949.

   The storms were Pacific.

   (**that / and / since**)

   _____

   _____

   _____

   _____

9. Some people might blame global warming for something.

   People blame global warming immediately.

   Global warming engenders so much hurricane activity.

   The activity is in such a short span.

   Hurricane center forecasters disagreed.

   (**while / for** / Change **engenders** to gerund form.)

   _____

   _____

   _____

10. They said something.

   Dean attained Category 5 status.

   Felix attained Category 5 status.

   Dean was nurtured by warm waters of the Caribbean.

   Felix was nurtured by warm waters of the Caribbean.

   Dean wasn't subjected to much wind shear.

   (that / and / because / and)

11. "It's not hard to set a record in any given year."

    The record is meteorological.

    Ed Rappaport said this.

    Ed Rappaport is the acting director of the hurricane center.

    (who)

12. Rappaport said something.

    "We shouldn't be that surprised to see hurricanes strengthen."

    "Hurricanes go through the Caribbean."

    (that / as)

13. The hurricane center started keeping tropical storm records.

    The storms were in the Atlantic.

    The center started keeping the records 156 years ago.

The center has recorded only Category 5 systems.

There were 12 Category 5 systems.

The systems were land-falling.

The systems were in this hemisphere.

The systems included Dean.

The systems included Felix.

(**since** / Change **included** to present participle form.)

_____

_____

_____

14. Three of those hit the United States.

    Two of those hit Florida.

    This includes the Labor Day hurricane.

    The Labor Day hurricane was in 1935.

    The Labor Day hurricane devastated the Keys.

    (Begin with **of those**. / **and** / Change **included** to present participle form. / **which**)

    _____

    _____

    _____

15. Hurricane Camille walloped Mississippi.

    This happened in 1969.

    Many people in still vividly remember Hurricane Andrew.

    Hurricane Andrew buzz-sawed through southern Miami-Dade County.

    This happened in 1992.

    (**and** / **which**)

    _____

    _____

    _____

16. Dean took the same generally westerly track.

    Felix took the same generally westerly track.

    There was a strong ridge of high pressure.

    The ridge was to the north.

    Forecasters said this.

    (and / because)

    _____

    _____

    _____

    _____

17. A hurricane specialist of the hurricane center cautioned something.

    The specialist was Jamie Rhome.

    Future storms might not follow suit.

    (that)

    _____

    _____

    _____

    _____

18. Felix became a rarity.

    Felix was by itself.

    It rapidly grew from a storm.

    The storm was a fledgling tropical storm.

    The storm grew to a Category 5 system.

    The storm grew in 42 hours.

    The storm set a record.

    The record was unofficial.

    Chris Landsea said this.

    Chris Landsea is the hurricane center's science officer.

Chris Landsea is the hurricane centers operations officer.

(**when** / Change **unofficial** to adverb form.)

_____

_____

19. Wilma was the previous holder of a distinction.

    Wilma happened in 2005.

    The distinction was unofficial.

    Wilma was growing from a tropical storm.

    The tropical storm was minimal.

    The tropical storm was growing to Category 5.

    It was growing in 48 hours.

    He said this.

    (**which**)

    _____

    _____

20. At 5 A.M. Eastern Daylight Time (EDT), Felix's center was "very near" Tegucigalpa.

    This happened on Wednesday.

    The hurricane center said something.

    Felix was moving westward.

    Felix was moving at 9 mph.

    (**;** / **that**)

    _____

    _____

21. William Gray is a hurricane prognosticator.

    Phil Klotzbach is a hurricane prognosticator.

William Gray is at Colorado State University.

Phil Klotzbach is at Colorado State University.

William Gray updated their seasonal forecast Tuesday.

Phil Klotzbach updated their seasonal forecast Tuesday.

William Gray was calling for three more hurricanes to form this month.

Phil Klotzbach was calling for three more hurricanes to form this month.

One of those was being a Category 3 or stronger.

(Begin with **meanwhile.** / **and** / **who** / **with**)

_____

_____

_____

22. They predict two more hurricanes.

    One of those is major.

    The hurricanes are to emerge in October.

    The hurricanes are to emerge in November.

    The hurricane season began on June 1.

    The hurricane season ends on Nov. 30.

    (**with** / Change **is** to **being.** / **which**)

_____

_____

_____

Notes for Grammar Points

Constructing Paragraphs Using Sentence Combining

Created by: Inès M. Mevs, M.S.Ed.

Fernando's Long Day

DIRECTIONS: Read the following simple sentences. Think about how you can combine two or more of these sentences into longer compound, complex, and compound-complex sentences. Then use your combined sentences to form a paragraph that is logical and cohesive. You may need to make changes, such as deleting certain words that are repeated, or using pronouns to replace certain nouns. Remember that one of your combined sentences will be the main idea of your paragraph, while the other sentences will be the supporting details. Don't forget to use the **COPS** rubric.

Fernando would like to forget all about yesterday.

Fernando got up late.

Fernando missed his bus.

Fernando finally got to school.

Fernando's locker was jammed.

Fernando was tardy to his first period class.

Fernando had an accident in the cafeteria during lunch.

Fernando dropped his tray.

Fernando got to science class.

Fernando realized something.

Fernando had forgotten his homework.

Fernando's grade was lowered.

The last bell rang to end school.

Fernando was ready to call it a day!

Fernando's Long Day

An Excellent Hobby

DIRECTIONS: Read the following simple sentences. Think about how you can combine two or more of these sentences into longer compound, complex, and compound-complex sentences. Then use your combined sentences to form a paragraph that is logical and cohesive. You may need to make changes, such as deleting certain words that are repeated, or using pronouns to replace certain nouns. Remember that one of your combined sentences will be the main idea of your paragraph, while the other sentences will be the supporting details. Don't forget to use **COPS**.

Tropical fish come in a great variety of shapes.

Tropical fish come in a great variety of sizes.

Tropical fish come in a great variety of colors.

They have a fascinating way of moving.

They have a fascinating way of feeding.

They have a fascinating way of breeding.

Tropical fish live in tanks.

The tanks can be an attractive feature.

The tanks can be in any room.

Tropical fish need care.

Care is far less than dogs.

Care is far less than cats.

These are a few reasons.

I recommend tropical fish as an excellent hobby.

An Excellent Hobby

Important People in School

DIRECTIONS: Read the following simple sentences. Think about how you can combine two or more of these sentences into longer compound, complex, and compound-complex sentences. Then use your combined sentences to form a paragraph that is logical and cohesive. You may need to make changes, such as deleting certain words that are repeated, or using pronouns to replace certain nouns. Remember that one of your combined sentences will be the main idea of your paragraph, while the other sentences will be the supporting details. Don't forget to use **COPS**.

There are two important people in a school.

The principal is one of the important people.

The student is one of the important people.

You might think something.

The principal is very different.

The student is very different.

In many ways the principal is alike.

In many ways the student is alike.

The student wants fair rules.

The principal wants fair rules.

The student wants the school to be an enjoyable place.

The principal wants the school to be an enjoyable place.

The student wants to learn.

The principal tries to see something.

The student can learn.

Most of all, the student wants something.

Most of all, the principal wants something.

Something is best overall for the student.

Important People in School

Annette

DIRECTIONS: Read the following simple sentences. Think about how you can combine two or more of these sentences into longer compound, complex, and compound-complex sentences. Then use your combined sentences to form a paragraph that is logical and cohesive. You may need to make changes, such as deleting certain words that are repeated, or using pronouns to replace certain nouns. Remember that one of your combined sentences will be the main idea of your paragraph, while the other sentences will be the supporting details. Don't forget to use **COPS**.

Annette was reading the newspaper want ads.

Annette wanted to find an after-school job.

Annette planned to earn some extra money.

Annette could buy a new CD player.

Annette's brother wanted a CD player.

The CD player was for Annette's brother's car.

Annette wanted to earn money soon.

Annette could earn money for a reason.

Good CD players are expensive.

The CD player would be a special surprise.

The surprise would be for Annette's brother's birthday.

Annette

Made in the USA
Lexington, KY
05 May 2011